Life During the Coronavirus Pandemic
Poems of Reality

By

Audrey M. Virges

Copyright ©2020 Audrey M. Virges

All rights reserved. No part of this publication may be reproduced, distributed, or transmitted in any form or by any means, including photocopying, recording, or other electronic or mechanical methods, without the prior written permission of the publisher, except in the case of brief quotations embodied in critical reviews and certain other noncommercial uses permitted by copyright law.

ISBN: 978-1-951300-12-8 Paperback
ISBN: 978-1-951300-16-6 eBook

Liberation's Publishing – West Point - Mississippi

Life During the Coronavirus Pandemic
Poems of Reality

By

Audrey M. Virges

Acknowledgement

I thank God for giving me the gift of writing poetry. Thanks to my family for their love and support. Thanks to those who have been an inspiration to me, and thanks to my church family and friends for their encouragement. Thanks to President Barack Obama and Michelle for sending me a card of thanks for a copy of my first book: *Living Reality.*

Audrey M. Virges

Table of Content

Introduction 11

What is COVID-19? 13

Symptoms of the Coronavirus 15

How COVID-19 Spreads 17

People Are Ill 19

No Vaccine 21

Larger Cities Hit by COVID-19 23

As COVID-19 Cases Rise All Over 25

On Their Job 27

Rooms and Ventilators Needed 29

Nursing Homes 31

COVID-19 and Children 33

So Many Lives Taken 35

Funeral Directors 37

Loved Ones Deserve More 39

Preventing the Spread 41

Buying Needed Supplies 43

Economy Shut Down 45

Schools Closed 47

School Graduation	49
Libraries Closed	51
Colleges Closed	53
Churches Closed	55
Job Shutdown	57
Obey the Lockdown Command	59
Gas Prices Down	61
Travel	63
Physical Contact	65
Stimulus Package	67
Buying Food	69
Afraid	71
Small Business	73
Bright Cities Are Dim	75
COVID-19 and the Homeless	77
No Place to Hide	79
COVID-19 and Depression	81
New Changes	83
The Pandemic Affected Tourism	85
Farmers	87

Life During the Coronavirus Pandemic

The C. D. C.. 89

The Economy Opened 91

God is Still In Charge 93

About the Author 95

Questionnaire 97

Audrey M. Virges

"There is Hope"

Life During the Coronavirus Pandemic

Introduction

We all go through calamities and devastating times
But not one like this that is so renown,
We've never in our generation seen a pandemic like this
One that shut the whole world down.

In the month of March 2020, the world was in shock
Learning of the horrific COVID-19 outbreak in all states,
The word was just being announced that this was a pandemic
That was going to cause lots of heartache.

COVID-19 is a mean and devastating disease
That's running rampant throughout the land,
It has no respect of persons or country
It will kill any woman, girl, boy, or man.

It is a very silent and deadly virus
So always we have to beware,
We have to exercise social distance and wear our masks
It could possibly be in the air.

The silent killer is taking lives daily
It's on the move taking people from their homes,
Exercising social distance will only allow burials, not funerals
And families are left to grieve alone.

We have to always be vigilant and stay in prayer
And stay as socially distant as we can be,
This is a monster that we can't handle
Only God can handle what we can't see.

Audrey M. Virges

"There is Hope"

Life During the Coronavirus Pandemic

What is COVID-19?

COVID-19 is very dangerous to your health
It is a coronavirus disease,
It is an upper respiratory tract illness
And it doesn't give your body ease.

Some people are asymptomatic
And do not know they have the disease,
Others experience the symptoms
And it is very hard for them to breathe.

The virus is silent and waiting
For someone for it to attack,
Two to fourteen days after you're exposed
You may be lying on your back.

So, practice social distance and wear your masks
And execute being as sanitary as you can,
This will really and truly help
To detour COVID-19's plan.

Audrey M. Virges

"There is Hope"

Life During the Coronavirus Pandemic

Symptoms of the Coronavirus

COVID-19 has its symptoms
Coughing is one alarm,
Whenever you cough
Remember to cough inside your arm.

Fever is a symptom
And so is shortness of breath,
Then you have to be put on a ventilator
As a means or possible prevention of death.

There's fatigue and muscle or body ache
Also, headache and loss of smell,
By the time you experience these things
You know you got it, and you really can tell.

Some people have a sore throat
Some have congestion and a runny nose,
You're then very well bent out of shape
From your head to your toes.

Some people have nausea and vomiting
And feel sick in their stomach and in their head,
The only thing left is to see the doctor
And then to be put to bed.

Audrey M. Virges

"There is Hope"

Life During the Coronavirus Pandemic

How COVID-19 Spreads

Droplets spread when someone cough
They also spread when they sneeze,
It's dangerous to be in the presence of someone
When they're infected with the COVID-19 disease.

Droplets also fall on surfaces
That someone will soon touch,
They will then touch their face
Which will create another COVID-19 case.

It's not a good thing to be too close to someone
To breathe in the air that they exhale,
That's why it is so important to social distance
That we will health wise prevail.

Audrey M. Virges

"There is Hope"

Life During the Coronavirus Pandemic

People Are Ill

So many people are now ill
And have no symptoms therein,
Everyone should be tested
To know if they should be quarantined in.

It is very dangerous to be out
Not knowing if you will infect someone,
It only takes being too close to someone
For the COVID-19 damage to be done.

Audrey M. Virges

"There is Hope"

Life During the Coronavirus Pandemic

No Vaccine

Scientist are working hard to find a COVID-19 vaccine
So far, no vaccine has been found,
They keep testing, and testing, and testing
Many times, over and around.

Maybe soon while testing
A breakthrough will come our way,
Because many COVID-19 patients
Are waiting on that day

Audrey M. Virges

"There is Hope"

Life During the Coronavirus Pandemic

Larger Cities Hit by COVID-19

People in larger cities are being devastated
Because they are so congested all around,
They walk so close together going to work
Every morning and evening going through town.

COVID-19 spreads fast in crowded places
It is its favorite breeding ground,
People must really exercise social distance
Then hopefully no cases will be found.

Audrey M. Virges

"There is Hope"

Life During the Coronavirus Pandemic

As COVID-19 Cases Rise All Over

As COVID-19 cases arise
Fear in our nation arise also,
We are hoping that this silent beast
Will soon be on the go.

It has brought so much turmoil
Into this world in which we live,
We are praying for God to heal the land
We hope it is His will.

Audrey M. Virges

"There is Hope"

Life During the Coronavirus Pandemic

On Their Job

Nurses and first responders are on the move
Working hard on double shifts,
Many of them are working in the larger cities
And they are moving ever so swift.

They put on their safety suits and go to work
Because of this pandemic they're in great demand,
They administer whatever help that's needed
And are always glad to do what they can.

When they do everything that can be done
To make the patients as comfortable as can be,
While keeping watch and assisting other patients
They are hoping for the victory.

Audrey M. Virges

"There is Hope"

Life During the Coronavirus Pandemic

Rooms and Ventilators Needed

There were not enough rooms for patients in hospitals
Other buildings were used for space,
There were also not enough ventilators
Orders were put in for more to be made.

There are patients very vulnerable to COVID-19
Because they are older in age,
The family thought they wouldn't make it
But they kept striving day by day.

Some lay there on ventilators helpless
There is nothing they could do,
To the family's surprise and God's grace
Some of them happily made it through.

Audrey M. Virges

"There is Hope"

Life During the Coronavirus Pandemic

Nursing Homes

As people age their immune system weakens
And their health begins to decline,
They begin to have underlying issues
That can so easily be defined.

COVID-19 is a devastating disease
That is so prevalent in nursing homes,
Older people are at a greater risk
So, they need to avoid exposure even if they're all alone.

They need to communicate with family every day
Because loneliness is devastating too,
It may not be so pleasing at the time
But it's doing what's best for them to do.

Audrey M. Virges

"There is Hope"

Life During the Coronavirus Pandemic

COVID-19 and Children

Children are a little less likely to contract COVID-19
But they can also get it too,
They also have to exercise social distance
Just like grownups have to do.

No more gathering and playing ball in the park
No more swimming together in the pool,
It's best to stay home and play video games
And chill out and play it cool.

Everyone has to social distance
From the oldest person to the small,
Let's make the children utilize that precaution
That goes for one and all.

Audrey M. Virges

"There is Hope"

Life During the Coronavirus Pandemic

So Many Lives Taken

COVID-19 has taken the lives of so many people
In different countries and in every state,
Families have lost their moms and dads
And many spouses lost their mates.

Many brothers and sisters passed away
And lots of next of kin,
Hopefully one day soon this pandemic will be over
And the bereaved, broken hearts will one day mend.

Audrey M. Virges

"There is Hope"

Funeral Directors

Funeral directors are in charge of so many burials
Little compassion to the bereaved can they show,
They want to put their arms around the family and comfort them
But because of social distance, that's not the way to go.

Families all over are hurting
Because the silent killer is on the rage,
For funeral directors, it's a burial again and again
It's the same book, just another page.

Audrey M. Virges

"There is Hope"

Life During the Coronavirus Pandemic

Loved Ones Deserve More

Loved ones deserve more than just to be buried
Because so many lives they have touched,
But because of COVID-19 on the rise
Funeral directors can only do so much.

Families would love for their loved ones
To have an inside church service for all to see,
And to have friends and loved ones come from different places
So, with their family they can be.

Shelter in place has great advantages
But it has a melancholy tone,
Because so many grieving families
Are left to grieve alone.

Audrey M. Virges

"There is Hope"

Life During the Coronavirus Pandemic

Preventing the Spread

There are ways to prevent the COVID-19 spread
Because prevention is a demand,
One way is to take precaution
And continually wash and sanitize our hands.

We should sanitize our homes and wear our masks and gloves
To protect our faces and hands,
To prevent the spread of COVID-19
That is so prevalent across this land.

We should stand six feet away from others
Wherever we may go,
Whether in the pharmacy or in a restaurant
Or in the grocery store.

Exercising measures of prevention is mandatory
It can save lives from day to day,
Let's be serious and help prevent the spread
To protect our lives in every way.

Audrey M. Virges

"There is Hope"

Life During the Coronavirus Pandemic

Buying Needed Supplies

Hand sanitizer is at the top of the list
Everyone is running to the store,
Stores are running out of supplies fast
While everyone is searching for more.

People used all their sanitizers at home
And needed more for themselves,
Lots of others were looking for tissue
But there were none left on the shelves.

Most all cleaning supplies were gone
None in the store not even in the box,
Very soon the shelves were clean
Of that good cleaning product Clorox.

There are many things we need
And we have to keep it straight,
There are some things we need
But we'll just have to wait.

Audrey M. Virges

"There is Hope"

Life During the Coronavirus Pandemic

Economy Shut Down

The economy is now shut down
And everything is quiet and still,
All restaurants are closed
Only a drive through to get your meal.

All jobs and businesses are shut down
For a while that's the way it has to be,
But Walmart and the grocery stores are open
And also, the pharmacy.

If we obey and exercise social distance
Things will be on the mend,
Then we can get back to our wonderful social life
And be happy and comfortable again.

Audrey M. Virges

"There is Hope"

Life During the Coronavirus Pandemic

Schools Closed

Schools are closed nationwide
To protect students, teachers, and the administration,
If COVID-19 attacks the school
Students and teachers would have no sense of concentration.

Millions of students in school rely on
School breakfast or lunch for food,
Schools gave out lunches every day
Which gave their parents a satisfying mood.

No matter what issues arise
There will be help along the way
To help keep people holding on each and every day.

Audrey M. Virges

"There is Hope"

Life During the Coronavirus Pandemic

School Graduation

Seniors spend twelve years in school
Studying hard to achieve their goals,
They are anticipating graduation day
So, they can wear their cap and gown so bold,

Every senior wants to be recognized
As they really and truly deserve to be,
They want to walk up and receive their diplomas
For all their friends and family to see.

COVID-19 came in and altered the plan
And caused some hesitation,
But some schools had a two-day ceremony
And some schools had a graduation drive through
But they still proudly had a graduation.

Audrey M. Virges

"There is Hope"

Life During the Coronavirus Pandemic

Libraries Closed

Using the library resources is a necessity
For patrons all around.
Books are checked out constantly
By people from the country and town.

Many people do not have access to a computer
Who use the computer at the library every day,
But now because of the pandemic, libraries are closed
And people have to find their own way.

Library week is really missed
And summer reading programs are missed too,
Patrons need the assistance of the librarian
To get their work done that they have to do.

Audrey M. Virges

"There is Hope"

Life During the Coronavirus Pandemic

Colleges Closed

Colleges are closed also
They're converting to online classes,
To keep students as safe as possible
Preventing them from being in great masses.

Parents have no desire to send their children
To live in heavily populated dorms,
Their desire is for them to be in a safe environment
So, their life will be the norm.

Audrey M. Virges

"There is Hope"

Life During the Coronavirus Pandemic

Churches Closed

No congregation meets inside the church anymore
No one is to gather inside,
The tithe box is set at the door
For everyone to come and pay their tithes.

Some churches gather in the parking lot
And for sure in their cars they sit,
The preacher preaches on the doorstep
Still trying to pull someone out of the pit.

What a blessing it will be when this pandemic is over
When everyone can assemble inside again,
Everyone will be praising God standing together
Waving and lifting their hands.

Audrey M. Virges

"There is Hope"

Life During the Coronavirus Pandemic

Job Shutdown

Workers are home on COVID-19 shutdown
Now their hard-working bodies can get some rest,
They know this situation won't last forever
And that it's really and truly a test.

Families can spend quality time together
While waiting on their unemployment checks,
They can take walks and play games with their children
And have family conversations on their decks.

Families can work a garden, fish, or ride horses
Or do whatever rejuvenate their mind,
It's good when they can kick back
And have quality family time.

Audrey M. Virges

"There is Hope"

Life During the Coronavirus Pandemic

Obey the Lockdown Command

While COVID-19 has caused a lockdown
Some people don't want to stay home,
Police are in place to enforce the command
That no one just ride around or roam.

Safety and social distance are great issues
So, everyone needs to stay in and mind,
Not obeying the command might get expensive
Because you might have to pay a fine.

Audrey M. Virges

"There is Hope"

Life During the Coronavirus Pandemic

Gas Prices Down

Gas prices really dropped at the pump
Which really made people smile,
With COVID-19 on the rise and everyone's staying in
People aren't driving many miles.

People are cautious where they go
No one can go to the mall anymore,
No one will go to a friend's house
Because very few will open their door

Audrey M. Virges

"There is Hope"

Life During the Coronavirus Pandemic

Travel

People love to travel to different places
But because the pandemic is on the rise,
That's not a very good idea
No one wants to compromise.

COVID-19 is worldwide
You can contract it anywhere,
On a bus, in a car, on a train, or in an elevator
As well as on a plane in the air.

You don't want to become ill
In a place far from home,
Being away from all your family and friends
You would feel so all alone.

Try not to travel unless it's a necessity
It may be tempting, but have a resistance,
Stay in and stay safe and healthy
And please exercise social distance.

Audrey M. Virges

"There is Hope"

Life During the Coronavirus Pandemic

Physical Contact

We have to avoid physical contact with others
Because COVID-19 does not play,
It's waiting for us to let our guard down
And give someone a simple warm embrace.

We have to get out of the norm
Of hugging people in which we care,
It's the norm for showing affection
And saying for you I care.

We have to avoid greeting someone in the store
Don't shake their hand, just nod your head,
We have to be careful
Because contracting COVID-19 we would really dread.

We have to condition our brains for social distance
And hang on and ride out the storm,
And pray that this pandemic is soon over
So, we can get back to the norm.

Audrey M. Virges

"There is Hope"

Life During the Coronavirus Pandemic

Stimulus Package

A stimulus package helps keep citizens going
And helps keep the economy from crashing too,
COVID-19 is a threat to our nation's wealth
And it's a bad threat to our health.

The stimulus package helps us buy food
And it helps us pay our bills where we lack,
It helps us to keep moving along
Until to our jobs we can make it back.

Audrey M. Virges

"There is Hope"

Life During the Coronavirus Pandemic

Buying Food

Lots of people are purchasing deep freezers
To store up lots of food for a while,
No one knows how long this pandemic will last
So, they're storing up can goods in piles.

Stores are announcing that higher prices are coming
From the next truck that comes in,
People need to buy now what grocery they can
To fill their freezer from end to end.

More people are planting gardens this year
To have extra food to store,
So, if there is a food shortage
They will have food for evermore.

Audrey M. Virges

"There is Hope"

Life During the Coronavirus Pandemic

Afraid

Regular sick people are afraid to go to the doctor
In fear of the virus they might get,
A few have been seriously ill
Hoping they would do well with the medicine they already got.

Fear of some kind lingers every day
Wondering if another wave will come,
No one knows how long this one will last
Because its course it will have to run.

Audrey M. Virges

"There is Hope"

Life During the Coronavirus Pandemic

Small Business

All businesses are closed because of this pandemic
Shutdown is the name of the game,
Small businesses are impacted greatly
They're trying to hang on and maintain.

Some small businesses caught a hold
Trying to help prevent the COVID-19spread,
They started to make masks for people to wear
Some hook around your ears, and some tie behind your head.

Masks are easy to make
They're worn in a safe manner,
If you don't have a bought or a homemade one
Just grab yourself a bandanna.

Audrey M. Virges

"There is Hope"

Life During the Coronavirus Pandemic

Bright Cities Are Dim

During the pandemic shutdown
Cities lost their allure,
Officials are wondering how long this will last
And also wondering how much the city can endure.

Four lane highways and a few cars now and then
No busses and trains to come around the bend.
No bright lights flashing because businesses are closed
Everyone is sheltered in place and staying indoors.

No one in the mall, no escalators going up and down
No children on the carousel to go around and around.
Everyone staying in and staying safe
No one wants COVID-19 without a doubt,

Shelter in place is what it is
There's nothing but the statues standing out.

Audrey M. Virges

"There is Hope"

Life During the Coronavirus Pandemic

COVID-19 and the Homeless

Shelter in place measures are being instituted worldwide
To all families and to the next of kin,
There are homeless people sleeping on the street
That have no homes to live in.

They are vulnerable and COVID-19 high risk
They lack the necessities to keep clean,
No food and no running water to wash their hands
And no family in which they can lean.

They have no job, no healthcare
And they are exposed to the environment,
They can't be sheltered in place
Because they have no money in which to pay rent.

There are some relief centers
That provide food, clothing, and water to wash their faces,
But there's no easy way for the homeless
To be sheltered in place.

Audrey M. Virges

"There is Hope"

Life During the Coronavirus Pandemic

No Place to Hide

The Covid-19 beast is everywhere
There's no place you can hide,
You can go up north, down south, out east, or out west
And there it will also abide.

Its name carries lots of sad fame
Because it is called everywhere,
It can and will destroy you quickly
Without a hint or a care.

It loves lots of company
And it loves to get in your face,
It will stay with you for a while
And you it will try to erase.

So always be aware of this virus
And abide by the shelter in place rules applied,
The virus is everywhere
And there is nowhere to hide.

Audrey M. Virges

"There is Hope"

Life During the Coronavirus Pandemic

COVID-19 and Depression

Many depressed people are mentally disturbed
And are calling the National Suicide Hotline,
Because of the trauma COVID-19 has caused
It has really taken a toll on their minds.

Mental health is an outstanding issue
That the nation is facing every day,
Some people can't take the pressure
Of becoming ill or losing a loved one the COVID-19 way.

Those people have to be encouraged that there's hope
Even in the times of isolation,
They must have therapy sessions
To love and embrace life and experience consolation.

Audrey M. Virges

"There is Hope"

Life During the Coronavirus Pandemic

New Changes

The pandemic made a difference
In the cities, country, and in the towns,
In the cities, the skies are much clearer
There are few drivers on the road
And less smog hanging around.

People in the country ride around eating
But shelter in place left them eating in their abodes,
No one will be angry when the shutdown is lifted
And they see no trash on the road.

Audrey M. Virges

"There is Hope"

Life During the Coronavirus Pandemic

The Pandemic Affected Tourism

Tourism has been affected by the pandemic
Because travel restrictions have been enforced,
The norm is for persons to travel where they want
But now they cannot travel like they choose.

Disney World is a great tourist attraction
During vacation, many people visit there,
They go to see the Disney characters
That they grew up watching on the air.

People prefer flying because it's a quick ride
Planes cut the time and fly with great power,
It doesn't take long to get where you're going
On a trip to see the Eiffel Tower.

Tourist attractions attract people far and near
As well as people from just around the bend,
They will be glad when people can return
And this pandemic comes to an end.

Audrey M. Virges

"There is Hope"

Life During the Coronavirus Pandemic

Farmers

Farmers are in a predicament
With nowhere to take their supply,
With stores and restaurants closed
No one to sell to; who can buy?

The shutdown caused a problem
And the farmers shut down their rigs,
They did not want to utilize euthanasia
Because they had an overcrowding of pigs.

Workers became ill with COVID-19
And the farmers shut their businesses down,
It brought about a shortage of food
That spiked higher prices in the stores in town.

Audrey M. Virges

"There is Hope"

Life During the Coronavirus Pandemic

The C. D. C.

The Center for Disease Control
Is working hard to prevent and control disease,
So, our nation can be healthy
And more people can be at ease.

They conduct research to let us know
That they try to protect our nation from health threats,
They are about saving the lives of our country
Then people can try to stay healthy yet.

Audrey M. Virges

"There is Hope"

Life During the Coronavirus Pandemic

The Economy Opened

The economy is gradually opening
All businesses are beginning to thrive,
Lots of people have gone back to work
And yet COVID-19 is still on the rise.

Large crowds are gathering at beaches
Other people are gathering at parties and bars,
Very few are wearing masks
And little social distancing is taking place by far.

Many football players are being quarantined
They are experiencing that the COVID-19 virus is real,
Baseball team players can socially distance while playing
But there will be no fighting on the field.

Different factories are up and running
Workers are making production giving it all they got,
But because of the crowded workplace
Some factories have become COVID-19 hotspots.

The workplace is what it is
It has to stay clean and sanitized all around,
Workers have to wear their masks

Audrey M. Virges

And social distance the best they can
To avoid another economy shutdown.

"There is Hope"

Life During the Coronavirus Pandemic

God is Still in Charge

This pandemic has really changed the world
From the way we've always known it to be,
People are wondering if this change will stick
Or if the world will snap back to reality.

We all want to get back to the world we knew
When we're comfortable in the presence of others,
When we can work, eat, travel, and worship together
And not be afraid to embrace one another.

Lots of changes have taken place because of COVID-19
We won't ever understand the changes of the world at large,
But no matter what changes take place
God is still in charge.

Audrey M. Virges

"There is Hope"

About the Author

I am Audrey M. Virges. I live in Woodland Ms. I was born and reared in Chickasaw County MS. I am married and we have three children and five grandchildren. I graduated from Houston High School, Houston Ms. And later received a bachelor's degree in Professional Interdisciplinary Studies at Jackson State University, Jackson, Ms. I am an artist. I am also employed at the Chickasaw County School District. I am very blessed to be a writer. My ability to write poetry is a gift from God, and my desire is to share my poems with the world.

Email: audreyvirges@yahoo.com
www.writeraudrey.virges.webs.com

Please visit my website and feel free to sign my guestbook page.

Audrey M. Virges

Life During the Coronavirus Pandemic

Questionnaire

1. What is COVID-19?

2. Name six symptoms of COVID-19

3. What month and year did COVID-19 begin to spread in all states?

4. Who are most vulnerable to COVID-19?

5. What should we do regularly because of COVID-19?

    A. Wash our clothes

    B. Wash our hands

    C. Wash our face

6. What are some COVID-19preventions?

    A. Wear masks

    B. Wash your hands

    C. Social distance

    D. All of the above

7. Where should you cough?

    A. Into the air

    B. Into your hand

    C. Inside your arm or in a tissue

8. COVID-19 spreads faster in what?

   A. Small towns

   B. Larger cities

   C. In the country

9. During the pandemic what kind of funerals did people have?

   A. They had funeral services inside of the church.

   B. They just had burials.

   C. They had the funerals at the funeral home.

10. A machine COVID-19 patient were put on to help them breathe.

    A. X-ray machine

    B. Exercise machine

    C. Ventilator

11. Money from the government to give aid to citizens in a pandemic.

    A. Income Tax

    B. Social Security

    C. Stimulus

Life During the Coronavirus Pandemic

12. Who works hard to prevent and control disease?

    A. MDOT

    B. Healthcare

    C. The C. D. C.

13. Is it a good time to travel during the pandemic?

    A. Yes

    B. No

14. Is it safe to visit people at their homes?

    A. Yes

    B. No

15. It is safe to greet someone with a hug during the pandemic.

    A. True

    B. False

16. It is not a good idea to store up food during the pandemic.

    A. True

    B. False

17. We should not wear our masks in a crowd.

    A. True

    B. false

Audrey M. Virges

18. Can we hide from COVID-19 in another state?

    A.   Yes

    B.   No

19. Who is the President of the United Stated during the Coronavirus Pandemic?

20. Who is Dr. Fauci?

21. Write an essay about the Coronavirus Pandemic.

Life During the Coronavirus Pandemic

Audrey M. Virges

www.ingramcontent.com/pod-product-compliance
Lightning Source LLC
Chambersburg PA
CBHW052113110526
44592CB00013B/1596